*To He that causes all things to be, my life is a humble "Thank you." To my husband Wayne for putting your precious energy into nurturing my dreams, and for my dear children Camille, Chrishanna and Carrington you are the period where there once was a question mark, I love you all.*

---

Copyright © 2011 Andrea Renee Frayser
All rights reserved. No part of this publication may be reproduced, distributed, or transmitted in any form or by any means without the prior written permission of the publisher.

ANDE Natural Products
21021 Black Rock Road
Hagerstown, MD 21740

ISBN: 0-615-45822X
ISBN:-9780615458229

## Table of Contents

Is The Pennywize Vegetarian for You?
The Four Food Groups for Vegetarians  6
The Well Stocked Pantry  7
Essential Kitchen Equipment  8
Money Saving Household Cleaning Options  9
Reduce Your Exposure to Food Borne Illness with These Simple Tips  10
Inexpensive Egg Alternatives for Baking  11
Creamy Soy Bean Milk  12
Soy Flour Milk  14
Soy "Butter Milk"  14
Easy Soy Yogurt  15
Vanilla Almond Milk  15

### Save Money with Soups, Chowders & Stews

Spinach Lentil Stew  16
Creamy Tomato Basil Soup  17
Luscious Vegan Corn Chowder  17
Speedy Taco Soup  18
Black Bean Soup  18

### Moderately Priced Main Dishes

Confetti Veggie Squares  19
Low Carb Pizza  19
Spinach Enchilada Bake  20
Whole Wheat Tortillas  20
Personal Pizza  21
Whole Wheat Pizza Crust  21
Rustic Cabbage & Cornbread Casserole  22
Easy Frank-n-Beans  22

### Quick Cheap & Easy Cold Dishes

Hoppin' John Salad  23
Corn & Black Bean Salad  23
Cucumber & Tomato Medley  24
Zesty Cranberry Slaw  24
Brown Rice Tabbouleh  25
Really Good Bruchetta  25
Next Generation Cobb Salad  26
Next Generation Cobb Salad Dressing  26
Tuscan Bread Salad  27
Basic Homemade Bread  27

# Is The Pennywize Vegetarian For You?

Have you ever wondered: "Why is the food that is good for my health bad for my budget?" or "Why does 'good- for- you- food' taste so bad?" Perhaps you want the benefits of eating a balanced vegetarian diet but the idea of existing on salads and tofu turns you off. Maybe you know you should be eating better, but don't know where to begin. If you can relate to *any* of these- this book is for you!

Many people jump on the vegetarian bandwagon for the health benefits, just to fall off from sticker shock. Let's face it, many of us want to eat better, but with the price of everything else going up– it is easier to skip the healthier choices "this time" with a promise to do better later.

I was faced with the same dilemma and found that by thinking out of the box-literally- I was able to feed my family of 5 for about ½ of what I was spending previously! That's right, I learned how to cut my food budget by half and eat healthier at the same time!

Not only did I improve my physical health (I lost over 60 pounds), but also my fiscal health (I used my budget surplus to pay down other bills) and you can too! I will share with you the secrets that I learned to save money without sacrificing our health. Are you ready for great tasting, budget friendly food along with tips for healthier living?  Then you need to get *The Pennywize Vegetarian* - you will be glad that you did.

# The Pennywize Vegetarian

Andréa Renée Frayser

## Economically Delicious Pasta Dishes

Vegan Pad Thai   28
Coconut Curried Couscous   29
Basic Marinara   29
Quick Fire Asian Citrus Noodles   30
The Perfect Pecan Pesto   30
Pasta with Pecan Pesto   31
Rachel's Bowtie Pasta   31
DIY Pasta   32

## Low-cost Adaptable Side Dishes

Pico de Gallo Corn   33
Summer Squash Medley   33
Green Bean d' Provence   34
Herbed Chick Peas   34
Creamy Coconut Rice   35
Spicy Malaysian Rice Sauce   35
Whole Wheat Corn Bread   36
Corn Bread Stuffing   36
Spicy Thai Noodles   37
Plantain Cake   37
Sweet & Sour Hodgepodge   38
Pecan Pesto Potatoes   38

## "Meaty" Vegetarian Dishes

Jamaican Pouches   39
Flaky Baked Empanada Dough   40
Jammin' Yam Casserole   40
A Bowl of Red   41
Big Momma Biscuits   41
Big Momma Biscuits & Sausage Gravy   42
Meatless Meatballs & Gravy   42

## Save Money By Making Your Own Snacks & Specialty Drinks

Veggie Chips   43
Tortilla Chips   43
Salsa de Patty   44
Creamy Coconut Bananas   44
Sticky Brown Rice with Mango   45
1-2-3 Peanut Butter Cookies   45
Black Bean Blender Brownies   46
Almond Masala Chai   46
Hibiscus Spritzer   47
Ginger Honey Tisane   47
**Resources**   48
**About The Author**   49
**A Note of Thanks**   50

# The Four Food Groups for Vegetarians

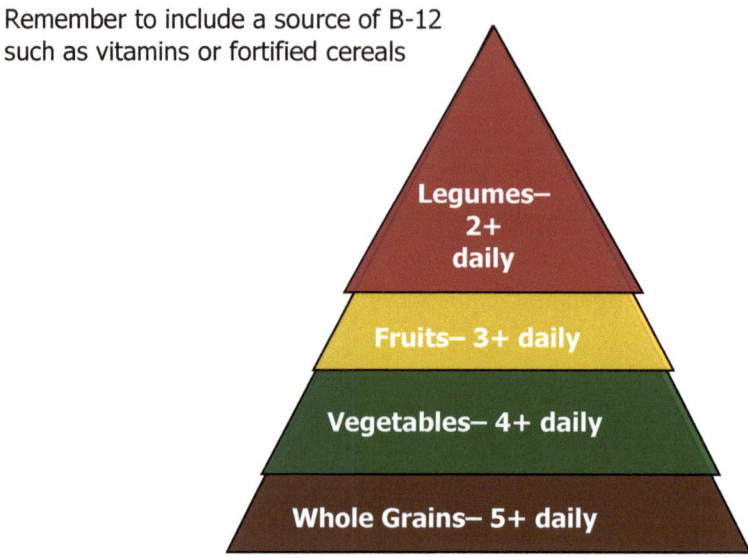

Remember to include a source of B-12 such as vitamins or fortified cereals

### Legumes- 2 or more servings daily
Consuming foods from this group is essential for building lean muscle and burning fat. Legumes include beans, peas and lentils and are an excellent source of protein, iron, calcium, zinc, fiber and B vitamins. Soymilk, tempeh, and Texturized Vegetable Protein (TVP) fall into this category. Examples: ½ cup cooked beans, 4 ounces of tofu, 8 ounces of soy milk

### Fruit- 3 or more servings daily
Fruits are rich in fiber, vitamin C, beta carotene and many other essential nutrients. Choose whole fruits over juices and stay alert to serving sizes. Examples: 1 medium piece of fruit, ½ cup cooked fruit or 4 ounces of juice

### Vegetables- 4 or more servings daily
Vegetables are packed with nutrients like riboflavin, calcium, fiber, iron, beta carotene and others. Strive to include a generous variety of these in your daily food choices. Look for dark rich colors, and buy fresh or frozen whenever possible. Examples: 1 cup raw vegetables, ½ cup cooked vegetables

### Whole Grains- 5 or more servings daily
Whole grains form the basis of so many meals and they are rich in fiber, protein, B vitamins, zinc, and complex carbohydrates. Foods such as cream of wheat, oat meal, corn, millet, barley, tortillas, bulgur, brown rice and whole grain pastas are included in this group. Examples: ½ cup hot cereal, 1 slice bread, and ½ cup cooked brown rice

# The Well Stocked Pantry

Keeping key items on hand is essential to controlling food costs and making healthier food choices. When choosing ingredients look for items that have the least amount of processing, such as raw sugar and whole wheat flour etc.

- ☐ Baking Powder (aluminum free)
- ☐ Baking Soda (aluminum free)
- ☐ Black Beans
- ☐ Black Pepper
- ☐ Bragg's Amino Acids
- ☐ Brown rice
- ☐ Canned or Jarred Tomatoes (Stewed, diced or whole)
- ☐ Cannellini Beans or other white beans
- ☐ Coconut Milk
- ☐ Cream of Mushroom Soup
- ☐ Cumin
- ☐ Dehydrated Onion Flakes
- ☐ Garlic Powder
- ☐ Italian Seasoning
- ☐ Kidney Beans or other Red Beans
- ☐ Powdered/ Boxed Milk (organic cow, soy, coconut, almond)
- ☐ Raw sugar
- ☐ Sea salt
- ☐ Season Salt (Non MSG)
- ☐ Soy Beans
- ☐ Soy Flour
- ☐ Texturized Vegetable Protein
- ☐ Unbleached All Purpose Flour
- ☐ Whole Wheat Flour
- ☐ Olive/ Vegetable Oil

The Pennywize Vegetarian

# **Essential Kitchen Equipment**

- Pastry Brush
- Rice Cooker
- Stainless steel bowls-a nesting set
- Strainer/ Colander
- Storage/ Freezer Bowls
- Kitchen towels, Flour Sack Towels and Cheese Cloth
- 2 Heat Resistant Rubber and one good metal spatula
- Metal cooking tongs
- Small ingredient dishes or cups
- Measuring spoons
- Wire whisk
- Vegetable Brush
- Veggie Wash see page 10 for DIY option
- Package of Plastic Hair Treatment/ Shower Caps—re-usable bowl covers
- Sauce Pots in two sizes – Stainless Steel, Cast Iron or Ceramic
- Frying or Sauté pans in two sizes- Stainless Steel, Cast Iron or Ceramic
- 3 Gallon Soup or Stock Pot
- 2 Cutting Boards- One plastic or wood, the other stone or solid surface
- Vegetable Peeler- OXO Soft Grips & Kyocera Ceramic Peelers are excellent choices
- Knives– ( US made Cutco knives are the best quality for your investment)
- Chef's 8 or 6 inch knife
- Paring knife
- Serrated or Bread knife
- Kitchenaid Mixer with attachments- Check the Kitchenaid site for sales and refurbished units
- Blender- The Blend Tec Blender is the blender of choice when you have funds to invest. It is powerful, easy to clean and blends just about anything including an I Pad. (Check out the You Tube "Will It Blend?" videos– amazing!)
- Immersion Blender– Viking is our preference. It makes creating soups, and gravies a snap with an easy clean up.

*A very special thanks to Kathleen Donovan of Cutco, Diane Humphrey of CookingEnthusiast.com and Karen Kaehler– Research Chef and ACF Certified Chef*

# Money Saving Household Cleaning Options

**Orange Spice Cleaner**: 1 Box baking soda, ½ teaspoon ground dried orange peel, ½ teaspoon cinnamon and ¼ teaspoon ground cloves. Mix together and store in an airtight container. Shake onto a damp surface and clean as usual. For stubborn stains, make into a paste and put it on the stain, let it sit overnight and wipe away in the morning. This may also be used as a toothpowder.

**Glass & Surface Cleaner:** ½ cup liquid castile soap and ½ cup water. Mix in a spray bottle use along with dry lint-free towels to clean glass.

**Fabric Softener:** Add one cup of vinegar to your washing machine to keep clothes soft. You can also dilute hair conditioner by 50% with water and wet a clean, lint-free cloth with it and toss it into the dryer to keep clothes static free.

**Color Safe Bleach:**
Airtight Plastic Container
2 cups Fels Naptha Soap, Zote or Ivory Soap (finely grated)
1 cup Washing Soda
1 cup Borax
-Mix well and store in an airtight plastic container.
-Use 2 tablespoons per full load.

**Homemade Laundry Soap (Gel):**
Large Plastic Pail with Lid (available in the paint department of most hardware stores)
1 quart Water (boiling)
2 cups Bar soap grated (Try Fell's Naptha, Zote or Ivory)
2 cups Borax
2 cups Washing Soda (found near the laundry soap in most stores, also available at hardware stores)

1. Add finely grated bar soap to the boiling water and stir until soap is melted. You can keep on low heat until soap is melted.
2. Pour the soap water into a large, clean pail and add the Borax and Washing Soda. Stir well until all is dissolved.
3. Add 2 gallons of water, stir until well mixed.
4. Cover pail and use 1/4 cup for each load of laundry. Stir the soap each time you use it as it will gel.

# Reduce Your Exposure to Food Borne Illness with These Simple Tips:

It is important to properly clean your fruits and vegetables before eating. Here are a few budget/ time friendly options...

**Castile Soap**: Dilute liquid castile soap 2 parts soap 1 part water and put it in a spray bottle. Spray fruits and vegetables with the mixture, scrub with a firm brush and rinse completely.

The Circle Brush

**Hydrogen Peroxide**: Spray hard to clean foods like grapes, broccoli, and cauliflower with hydrogen peroxide and let set for 3-5 minutes. Rinse thoroughly.

**Potato Gloves**: These not only do an amazing job cleaning potatoes but also carrots, beets and other root vegetables. Just put them on, rinse and scrub. It is that easy!

On the go? **Eat Cleaner wipes** are a must have! Keep some in your purse, desk and car, and make sure your kids have some available for school. You can wipe your food clean without leaving harmful residue. They are also great for cleaning your hands before eating.
**www.eatcleaner.com**

# Inexpensive Egg Alternatives for Baking

*There are many reasons people want to avoid eggs, from controlling cholesterol to questions about safety. Whatever the reason, you will find the following very helpful.*

---

For Light Colored baked goods like yellow cake this recipe **replaces two whole eggs:**
Sift Together:
1 Tbsp tapioca or corn starch
1 Tbsp potato starch
1/4 tsp baking powder
1/8 tsp xanthan gum (optional)
Add 1/2 cup water and 2 tsp oil.
Whisk until thoroughly combined and somewhat frothy add to recipe immediately.

---

For Dark Colored items such as cookies and brownies that benefit from a nutty flavor:
2 Tbsp. Finely ground flax seeds plus 3 Tbsp. water **replaces one egg**. Mix them together in a small bowl or mug, and let sit a couple of minutes until it becomes like jelly, then add to recipe.

---

For Quick breads, Pancakes, Muffins and Cakes:
1/4 cup Soy Yogurt **replaces 1 egg**
1/2 Ripe Banana blended until smooth **replaces 1 egg**

---

For Dense Foods like Brownies, Cakes and Sweetbreads:
1/4 cup Blended Silken Tofu **replaces 1 egg**
1/4 cup Applesauce also works in a variety of situations as a **replacer for one egg.**

1 TBS wet/ raw okara (soy pulp from soybean milk production) + 2 TBS water **replaces 1 egg**

*Look for great deals on food in unexpected places. Discount stores like Ross, Tuesday Morning or Big Lots often get close outs on high-end and organic foods which they sell for a small fraction of their retail price!*

# Creamy Soy Bean Milk

*Soy milk is a great alternative to animal milk. It provides essential proteins to the vegetarian diet, this recipe contains 5.5 % protein compared to 3% for dairy milk and can cost about 24 cents a batch!*

**Ingredients:**

1 Cup Soybeans- soaked in 2 quarts water overnight rinsed and drained twice
1 Tablespoon Rolled Oats
2 Tablespoon Raw Sugar, Honey or Agave Nectar (Optional)
1/2 teaspoon Sea Salt
4 Cups Water (approximately)

Special Equipment:
Blender
Cheesecloth
Large Heat-proof Bowl
Rubber Spatula
Glass Jar or Potato Masher
Cooking Pot

---

**Directions:**

1. Combine soybeans, oatmeal and 2 2/3 cup water in a blender and puree at high speed for 3 minutes.
2. Add puree to cooking pot, and heat to medium high, stirring the bottom constantly to prevent sticking.
3. When the foam suddenly rises in the pot, remove it from the heat.
4. Pour the puree into the cheese cloth that is draped in the heat-proof bowl.
5. Rinse pot out and set it aside.
6. Allow the mixture to cool in the bowl and then twist the cheesecloth closed and press it against the side of the bowl, using the jar, or masher to remove any additional milk.
7. Return milk to the pot and bring it back to a boil over medium heat. Stir constantly to prevent sticking reduce heat and cook for 7 minutes.
8. Add the sugar, honey, or agave nectar and sea salt.

May be used or cold.


*Store brands are often the same as their "name brand" counterparts but the store enters in to a special agreement to have their "private label" placed on the product. Compare ingredients, you may be surprised at how much you can save!*

# The Pennywize Vegetarian

13

## Soy Flour Milk

**Ingredients:**

1 Cup Organic Soy Flour
1 Tablespoon Rolled Oats
2 Tablespoons Honey* or Raw Sugar
3 Cups Water
Rubber Spatula
Cheese Cloth
Heat-proof bowl
Potato Masher or Glass Jar
Heat-proof jar for storage

**Directions:**
1. Combine soy flour, rolled oats, honey or sugar and 3 cups of water in a small saucepan and bring to a boil over medium heat, stirring constantly.
2. When foam suddenly rises in the pot, quickly remove from heat and pour the contents of the pot into the cheese cloth that is draped in the bowl.
3. Using a rubber spatula remove any remaining puree from the pot and place it in the cheesecloth. (Wash the pot-you will need it again.)
4. Twist the cheesecloth closed and with the masher or the glass jar, press it against the side of the bowl to remove any additional milk.
5. Return the milk to the clean cooking pot and bring to a boil over medium heat. Stir constantly to prevent sticking reduce heat and cook for 7 minutes.
6. Serve hot or cold.
*May be stored in the refrigerator for up to a week.

## Soy "Butter Milk"

**Ingredients:**

1 Cup Soymilk
1 teaspoon Vinegar or Lemon Juice

**Directions:**
1. Combine ingredients in a cup.
2. Let sit for 15 minutes until milk becomes thick.

## Easy Soy Yogurt

**Ingredients:**

3 1/4 cup homemade soymilk
1 teaspoon soymilk yogurt*
Clean Glass Jar
* May be commercially purchased yogurt to start, however; you may wish to reserve some of your first batch for subsequent recipes

---

**Directions:**
1. Allow freshly made soymilk to cool to 105 degrees, removing the film that forms.
2. Stir in the yogurt and pour the mixture into the glass jar.
3. Cover and allow to stand at room temperature for 14-18* hours.
4. Serve as is or sweeten with a little honey, agave nectar, fruit, or serve with granola.

*The subtle tang and sourness of yogurt will not develop and if cultured too long, it will separate into curds and whey.*

## Vanilla Almond Milk

**Ingredients:**

1 to 1 ½ cups of raw almonds
4 cups of filtered or spring water
3-8 dates
1 teaspoon vanilla extract

---

**Directions:**
1. Soak almonds and dates in water for at least six hours.
2. Drain soaked almonds, and dates and blend with 4 cups of fresh water until you get a milk-like consistency. Add the vanilla extract.
3. Strain to remove granules and store in an airtight container for up to a week.

*The internet can be a source of great food deals, check out: Ebay, Craigslist, Amazon, Freecycle as well as "bulk" sellers.*

## Save Money with Soups, Chowders & Stews

*What can you do when you have a little bit of a lot of ingredients but they are not enough to satisfy your family's hunger? Add a lot of herbs, seasonings and fluid and make it into a delicious filling soup. Soups are a good way to stretch your family's dollar while satisfying their hunger. Plus there is something so comforting about a nice bowl of soup. Try these recipes out and I know that you will agree!*

## Spinach Lentil Stew

**Ingredients:**
½ cup chopped onion
4 cloves garlic minced
2 Tablespoons vegetable oil
2 cups dried lentils
1 Tablespoons dried thyme
½ teaspoon black pepper
2 teaspoon season salt– MSG free
½ teaspoon cumin
1 ¼ cup chopped carrots
7 cups water (divided 5 cups/ 2cups)
1 (14.5 oz) can diced tomatoes (un-drained)
1 (10 oz) package of spinach (fresh or frozen)
Sea salt to taste
1 Tablespoon red wine vinegar

**Directions:**
1. In a large saucepan sauté onion, garlic and lentils for 2 minutes.
2. Add the thyme, black pepper, season salt and cumin.
3. Mix thoroughly and add 5 cups of water.
4. Bring to a boil and reduce heat.
5. Cover and simmer for 30 minutes.
6. Add the carrots, tomatoes and spinach. Return to a boil.
7. Reduce heat, cover and simmer for 15-20 minutes longer until lentils are tender.
8. You may need to add as much as 2 more cups of water to keep the soup from drying out during cooking.
9. Stir in red wine vinegar.

*Look to "ethnic" grocers for incredible savings on herbs, spices and fresh produce.*

## Creamy Tomato Basil Soup

**Ingredients:**
4 cups ripe tomatoes chopped
¼ cup fresh basil leaves chopped
2 large cloves of garlic crushed
2 Tablespoons olive oil
1 cup organic soy milk (plain)
2 teaspoons sea salt
½ Teaspoon black pepper

**Directions:**
1. In a large sauce pan heat olive oil and garlic.
2. Add tomatoes, basil, and salt to the pot and cook tomatoes until they begin to break down.
3. Add the soy milk and simmer for 10 minutes.
4. Remove from heat and cool for 5 minutes.
5. Transfer soup to a blender and pulse to smooth or use an emulsion blender.
6. Serve warm or freeze for later use.

## Luscious Vegan Corn Chowder

**Ingredients:**
2 Tablespoons olive oil
3 cloves of garlic chopped
1 cup onion chopped
1 cup roasted bell pepper chopped
4 cups whole kernel corn
14 oz can coconut milk
4oz organic soy milk (plain)
4 teaspoons curry powder
2 teaspoons dried basil
1 Tablespoon season salt– MSG free
1/2 teaspoon black pepper
1 teaspoon sea salt
2 Tablespoons corn starch dissolved in 1/2 cup warm water

**Directions:**
1. Heat oil in a large saucepan over medium heat.
2. Add garlic and onion. Heat until tender.
3. Add roasted red pepper, corn, and seasonings heating thoroughly.
4. Add coconut and soy milks and cook until corn is tender.
5. Add the corn starch mixture stirring constantly and return to boil.
6. Cook until thickened and remove from heat.

## Speedy Taco Soup

**Ingredients:**
2-15 oz cans of black beans
1-15 oz can of butter beans
1-15 oz can of corn
1-15 oz can of diced tomatoes
1-1.25 oz taco seasoning mix
2 Tablespoons dehydrated onions
2 teaspoons cumin
tortilla chips for garnish
plain soy yogurt (optional)

**Directions:**
1. Combine all of the ingredients in a saucepan and simmer for 15 minutes.
2. Sprinkle with tortilla chips and/or soy yogurt to garnish.

## Black Bean Soup

**Ingredients:**
2- 15 oz cans black beans
1- 15 oz can stewed tomatoes- diced
1 Tablespoon olive or vegetable oil
1 Tablespoon cumin
1 Tablespoon oregano
1 Tablespoon dehydrated onion
1 cup onion, diced large
1/2 cup red pepper, diced large
1/2 green pepper, diced large
6 cloves garlic, chopped
1 teaspoon sea salt

**Directions:**
1. In a large sauce pan, heat oil over medium heat.
2. Add, the garlic, onion, and peppers, and cook until tender, about 4 minutes.
3. Add the diced stewed tomatoes, and heat for another 2 minutes.
4. Add the black beans, cumin, oregano, dehydrated onions, and sea salt.
5. Reduce heat and simmer for 10 minutes.

*Enjoy deep savings on herbs and spices over the grocery store prices by buying them at Dollar or "Lot" Stores.*

## Moderately Priced Main Dishes

Whether for lunch, brunch or dinner these fantastic recipes are very satisfying, surprisingly easy and inexpensive to make.

## Confetti Veggie Squares

**Ingredients:**
2 TBS olive oil or vegetable oil
1 cup whole wheat flour
1 tsp baking powder
3/4 tsp sea salt
3 tsp Italian seasonings
1/4 tsp black pepper
3 eggs
1 cup organic soy milk
2-10 ounce packages frozen chopped spinach (thawed and squeezed dry)
2 cups shredded cheddar cheese
2 cups shredded Monterey Jack cheese
1 cup onion chopped
1/2 cup roasted red peppers chopped

**Directions:**
Preheat oven 350
1. Brush bottom and sides of 13"x9" dish with oil and set aside.
2. In a large bowl combine remaining ingredients and mix well.
3. Spread into prepared pan.
4. Bake uncovered for 30-35 minutes until a toothpick inserted in center comes out clean and edges are slightly brown.

## Low Carb Pizza

**Ingredients:**
1/4 cup sliced tomatoes
1/2 cup fresh spinach
1/3 cup sliced onions
1/4 cup tomato sauce
1/2 teaspoon Italian seasoning
sea salt & black pepper (to taste)

**Directions:**
Preheat oven 350
1. In a small oven-proof dish toss the tomatoes, spinach, onions, sauce and seasoning until well mixed.
2. Top with cheese and bake until the cheese begins to brown.

## Spinach Enchilada Bake

**Ingredients:**
2 Tablespoons olive oil
1 cup onion chopped fine
3 cloves garlic
1 cup mushrooms chopped fine
2 -10 oz packages frozen spinach thawed and squeezed dry
2 teaspoons Italian seasoning
1 teaspoon sea salt
3/4 teaspoon black pepper
6- 7" whole wheat tortillas (see recipe below)
3 cups salsa
2 cups Mexican blend cheese

**Directions:**
Preheat oven to 350
1. In a medium sized pan, heat the oil, add garlic, onion and spinach cook until soft.
2. Add the Italian seasoning, sea salt and black pepper.
3. In a baking dish, layer salsa, tortillas, spinach mixture, and cheese alternating until you use all the ingredients ending with the cheese.
4. Bake until cheese is bubbly and browning.

## Whole Wheat Tortillas

**Ingredients:**
1 cup unbleached flour
1 cup whole wheat flour
1 teaspoon sea salt
1 teaspoon baking powder
4 tablespoons olive or vegetable oil
2/3 cup water

**Directions:**
1. Combine flours, baking powder and sea salt, make a well in the center.
2. Stir in the oil and water with fork.
3. When dough can be gathered into a small ball, turn out onto a floured surface a knead a few times.
4. Form 8 balls of dough, and cover with a clean damp towel until ready to use.
5. Flatten ball into a disk and then roll out on a floured surface until 7 inches or larger with even strokes that do not reach out to the edge. Remember to turn over frequently.
6. Place tortilla in ungreased preheated (medium heat) frying pan.
7. Cook 30 to 40 seconds on each side turning with a spatula.
8. The first side should be pale and sprinkled with brown spots, the second side will be blotched.
9. Stack tortillas on a plate and cover with a clean damp cloth to keep them soft.
10. Repeat process with remaining dough.

## Personal Pizza

**Ingredients:**
4 prepared pizza crusts– recipe below
1 cup sliced onions
1 cup sliced bell peppers
1 cup sliced tomatoes
1/2 cup fresh basil
2 cups Marinara Sauce– recipe on page 29
3-4 cups cheese of choice
sea salt (to taste)
black pepper (to taste)
red pepper flakes (optional)

**Directions:**
Preheat oven to 400 degrees.
1. Place 1/4 cup Marinara Sauce on each pizza crust. Add toppings and cheese.
2. Sprinkle with sea salt, pepper, basil, peppers (optional) and cheese.
3. Place on a cookie sheet and bake until cheese is slightly browned and bubbly.

## Whole Wheat Pizza Crust

**Ingredients:**
2 cups whole wheat flour
1 1/2 cup unbleached flour
1/2 teaspoon sea salt
2 teaspoon Instant yeast
2 Tablespoon molasses (vegan choice) or honey
1/4 cup olive or vegetable oil
1 cup warm water

**Directions:**
1. In a large bowl mix flours, sea salt and yeast. Make a well in the center.
2. Add the molasses/ honey, olive oil and water. Mix to form a firm silky dough.
3. Remove the dough from the bowl and knead until completely mixed and elastic.
4. Oil bowl and return dough to the bowl and cover with plastic wrap and a clean damp dishcloth.
5. Set in a warm location to double in size. (About an hour)
6. Divide into two (or more) equal parts and roll into a ball.
7. Place ball on a lightly floured surface and roll out to desired size.
8. Top as desired.

## Rustic Cabbage & Cornbread Casserole

**Ingredients:**
1 Tablespoons (3 cloves) garlic chopped
2 Tablespoons vegetable or olive oil
3/4 cup onion sliced
1 cup bell peppers sliced
1 cup carrots sliced
8 cups cabbage (1 small head)
2 teaspoons season salt– MSG free
2 teaspoons oregano
1/2 teaspoon black pepper
2 cups (or 1- 15 oz can) cream of mushroom soup
1 batch of Whole Wheat Corn Bread Batter– recipe on page 36

**Directions:**
Preheat oven to 400 degrees
1. In a large saucepan heat oil, garlic, onions, bell peppers, carrots, cabbage and seasonings over medium heat for 5 minutes stirring occasionally.
2. Add the soup and mix well.
3. Transfer cabbage to a casserole dish- distributing it evenly.
4. Pour on the premade Whole Wheat Cornbread batter, distributing it evenly.
5. Bake until cornbread is brown and completely cooked. About 30 minutes.

## Fast & Easy Frank-n-Beans

**Ingredients:**
4 Yves ® Meatless Hotdogs sliced
1/2 cup chopped onion
1/2 cup chopped peppers
1- 28 oz can Bush's Vegetarian Baked Beans
1/2 teaspoon sea salt
1/4 teaspoon black pepper

**Directions:**
1. Add all of the ingredients into a large pan and heat through.
2. Simmer for 5 minutes and serve.

*How many times have you seen fruit fallen from a tree and laying on the ground rotting? Why not ask the homeowner if they would allow you to purchase a few baskets full if you pick it? It saves them the hassle and you money!*

## Quick Cheap & Easy Cold Dishes

More than just salads (although there are some fabulous salad recipes in this section) cold dishes are a great choice for those who want to save money by carrying lunch.

## Hoppin' John Salad

**Ingredients:**
1 cup bulgur wheat (prepared according to package directions)
4 cups cooked black eyed peas
1/2 cup onions chopped
1 cup bell peppers chopped
2 teaspoons garlic powder
1 teaspoon sea salt
1/2 teaspoon black pepper
2 Tablespoons Italian seasonings
2 teaspoon season salt– MSG free
4 Tablespoons balsamic vinegar
2 Tablespoons olive oil

**Directions:**
1. Combine the ingredients in a large bowl and mix well.
2. Serve chilled.

## Corn & Black Bean Salad

**Ingredients:**
4 cups frozen corn (thawed)
2 (14 oz) cans black beans drained and rinsed
2 cups chopped tomatoes
1/2 cup fresh cilantro chopped
juice of 2 limes
2 teaspoons garlic powder
1 teaspoon cumin
1 teaspoon chili powder
1 teaspoon sea salt
1/2 teaspoon black pepper

**Directions:**
1. Combine ingredients in a large bowl and mix well.
2. Let marinate for 30 minutes to an hour before serving.

## Cucumber & Tomato Medley

**Ingredients:**
4 cups sliced cucumbers
2 cups sliced tomatoes
1 cup chopped onion
1 1/2 teaspoon sea salt
1/2 teaspoon black pepper
1 Tablespoon Italian seasoning
4 Tablespoons apple cider vinegar

**Directions:**
1. In a large bowl combine all ingredients and mix well.
2. Refrigerate for 30 minutes to marinate.

## Zesty Cranberry Slaw

**Ingredients:**
8 cups cabbage shredded
2 cups carrots shredded
1 cup diced onion
1/2 cup shredded red bell pepper
1 cup chopped mixed nuts
1 1/2 cup dried cranberries
8 Tablespoons red wine vinegar
4 Tablespoons olive oil
1 teaspoon black pepper
1 Tablespoon fresh ginger chopped
1 Tablespoon Italian seasoning
1 teaspoon garlic powder
1 teaspoon season salt*
1/2 teaspoon hot pepper flakes
1/4 teaspoon allspice
2 teaspoons sea salt
1 teaspoon raw sugar

*Photo Courtesy of Todd Price whose wife, Kim, loves this recipe! Thanks!*

\* MSG– free

**Directions:**
In a large bowl, combine all of the ingredients and mix thoroughly.

*Freeze single servings of leftovers to use for "fast food" when you are short on time. Be sure to label the contents and the date. Discard any unused food after 6 months.*

## Brown Rice Tabbouleh

**Ingredients:**
1 cup brown rice
2 cups water
½ teaspoon sea salt
¼ cup olive or grape seed oil
½ teaspoon sea salt
¼ cup fresh lime juice
1 cup fresh parsley chopped
½ cup fresh mint chopped
1 cup tomatoes diced
¾ cup cucumber diced
1 cup diced green onions
1 cup grated carrots
1 head of Romaine lettuce separated into leaves
toasted pitas (Optional)

**Directions:**
1. In a saucepan over medium heat, combine the brown rice, water and ½ teaspoon sea salt, bring to a boil.
2. Reduce heat and cover.
3. Cook until water is absorbed and rice is fully cooked, about 20 minutes.
4. In a large bowl, mix oil, sea salt, lime juice, parsley and mint.
5. Add tomatoes, cucumber, green onions and carrots and toss well.
6. Add the cooled brown rice and mix thoroughly.
May be served immediately with romaine lettuce "cups" or toasted pitas.

## Really Good Bruchetta

**Ingredients:**
4 cups chopped tomatoes
1 Tablespoon olive oil
1/2 cup loosely packed fresh basil
2 cloves garlic chopped
1/2 teaspoon sea salt
1/4 teaspoon black pepper
1 teaspoon Italian seasonings
4 oz sliced mozzarella cheese for garnish

**Directions:**

1. In a large bowl combine all ingredients and mix well.
2. Let set for 20 minutes before serving.
3. Spoon on top of toasted bread and garnish, if desired, with cheese.

## Next Generation Cobb Salad

**Ingredients:**
2 Chix Tenders cooked &diced
1 cup chopped romaine lettuce
1 cup chopped spinach
2 Tablespoons crumbled blue cheese
2 Tablespoons imitation bacon bits
2 Tablespoons tomatoes diced
2 Tablespoons chopped fresh chives
1 hardboiled egg diced
1/4 avocado diced
Cobb Salad Dressing– see recipe below

**Directions:**
1. Place lettuce and spinach on a plate.
2. Arrange diced Chix tenders, blue cheese, bacon bits, tomatoes, egg, chives and avocado in rows on the bed of lettuce and spinach.
3. Drizzle with Cobb Salad Dressing immediately before serving.

## Next Generation Cobb Salad Dressing

**Ingredients:**
1 teaspoon Dijon mustard
2 medium cloves garlic
¼ teaspoon raw sugar or agave nectar
½ teaspoon sea salt
1/8 teaspoon black pepper
½ teaspoon tamarind paste
½ teaspoon Bragg's Amino Acids
2 teaspoon lemon juice
2 TBS red wine vinegar
½ cup extra virgin olive oil
Dash hot pepper sauce

**Directions:**
Combine ingredients in a blender or food processor until completely blended.

Will keep in the refrigerator for up to a week.

*Beware of hidden animal ingredients! Worchester Sauce, vegetable Soup, prepared stuffing, flavored rice and marshmallows are all items that commonly contain hidden animal ingredients.*

The Pennywize Vegetarian

## Tuscan Bread Salad

**Ingredients:**
1 Tablespoon extra- virgin olive oil
1 clove of garlic peeled
4 slices (1/2-inch thick) bread
6 Cups Romaine lettuce torn
1/2 cup drained black olives, halved
1 large ripe tomato, seeded and diced
1 cup canned Great Northern or cannellini beans, drained and rinsed
3 Tablespoons extra-virgin olive oil
1 cloves garlic, minced
2 tablespoons balsamic vinegar
1/2 teaspoon sea salt
1/2 teaspoon black pepper
2 tablespoons fresh basil leaves, sliced

**Directions:**
Preheat oven to 375
1. Place bread on a cookie sheet and drizzle the pieces with the olive oil.
2. Rub each slice with the peeled garlic and bake until nicely toasted.
3. In a bowl, combine lettuce, olives, tomato and beans.
3. Cut toasted bread into cubes and add to the lettuce mixture.
4. Combine the 3 tablespoons oil, minced garlic, balsamic vinegar, sea salt and pepper; mix well. Add to lettuce mixture; toss well.
3. Sprinkle cut basil over the top of salad and serve.

## Basic Homemade Bread

**Ingredients:**
2 cups wheat flour
1 1/2 cups unbleached flour
1 teaspoon sea salt
2 teaspoons instant yeast
1 1/3 cup warm water

**Directions:**
1. In a large bowl mix 2 cups wheat flour, the yeast, salt and water together.
2. Slowly mix in enough of the remaining flour to form a firm moist dough.
3. Turn dough onto a lightly floured work surface and knead until smooth and elastic. (About 10 minutes)
4. Oil a clean bowl and place the dough inside.
5. Cover the top of the dough with plastic wrap and a clean damp dishtowel.
6. Let rise until double the size (1-2 hours) punch down and let rest for 10 minutes.
7. Shape dough into a long loaf and place on a floured baking sheet, covering with a dish towel. Let double in size. (45 minutes)
8. Cut 5 diagonal slashes across the top of loaf and bake in a preheated oven at 425 for about 45 minutes. (Loaf should be golden and sound hollow when tapped).
9. Cool on a wire rack.

## Economically Delicious Pasta Dishes

Pasta is an inexpensive and flexible option for better eating if you choose whole grain pastas. By choosing whole grain pastas you optimize the nutritional value of your entire meal.

## Vegan Pad Thai

**Ingredients:**
6 Tablespoons of crunchy peanut butter
4 Tablespoons water
3 Tablespoons vegetable oil
3 Tablespoons sesame oil
3 Tablespoons rice vinegar
4 Tablespoons Braggs Aminos
4 Tablespoons tamarind paste
1 Tablespoon raw sugar or agave
1 1/2 Tablespoon minced ginger root
1 1/2 Tablespoons minced garlic cloves
1 Tablespoon chili paste
1 - 16 oz package of whole grain spaghetti
Garnish:
bean Sprouts
cilantro
Lime

**Directions:**
1. Prepare pasta according to package directions.
2. While the pasta is cooking, place another saucepan on low heat and mix together the peanut butter and the water. You should have a soupy peanut butter mixture in the pan.
3. Add the vegetable oil, sesame oil, rice vinegar, aminos, tamarind, and sugar/ agave, stirring well after each ingredient. If the mixture begins to boil, reduce the heat and stir well.
4. Add the ginger root, garlic and chili paste and heat to bubbling, and instantly remove from heat and stir.
5. Let the sauce set for a two minutes.
6. Add to drained pasta and mix well.
7. Garnish as desired with bean sprouts, cilantro and lime.

*It is easy to recycle vegetable peelings into delicious soup stock. Use 1 cup of vegetable scraps to 5 cups water, add sea salt, black pepper and herbs of your choosing. Boil 30 minutes , remove from heat and strain. You can freeze this for up to a year .*

## Coconut Curried Couscous

**Ingredients:**
2 Tablespoons olive oil
2 cloves garlic chopped
1 cup diced potatoes
1/2 cup pecans chopped
1/2 cup dried cranberries
1/2 cup diced bell peppers
2 Spring onions diced
1 1/2 teaspoon sea salt
1/2 teaspoon black Pepper
2 teaspoons dried cilantro
2 teaspoons dried thyme
1 teaspoon basil
1 cup frozen peas & carrots
2 cups couscous
1- 13 oz can coconut milk
1 1/2 cup water
1/2 cup toasted coconut– see instructions on page 44

**Directions:**
1. In a large pan heat olive oil, garlic, potatoes, pecans, cranberries, bell peppers and onions for 10 minutes or until peppers and potatoes are soft.
2. Add the sea salt, black pepper, cilantro, thyme, basil and the frozen peas and carrots and cook for three minutes.
3. Add the couscous, coconut milk and water, Cook until fluid is absorbed.
4. Remove from heat and fluff couscous. Top with toasted coconut.

## Basic Marinara

**Ingredients:**
2 tablespoons extra-virgin olive oil
3 large cloves garlic, minced
2 medium onions, coarsely chopped
4 cups chopped tomatoes
3 Tablespoons Italian seasonings
1 ½ teaspoon sea salt- to taste
½ teaspoon black pepper

**Directions:**
1. In a large sauce pan, heat the olive oil to medium.
2. Add the garlic, onions, tomatoes, the Italian seasoning, black pepper, and sea salt. Cook until the tomatoes break down (about 25 minutes).
3. Finish by blending with an emulsion blender or by placing the sauce in a food processor.

## Quick Fire Asian Citrus Noodles

**Ingredients:**
1 teaspoon chili flakes
12 oz package of Udon noodles
1 cup orange juice (fresh preferred)
¼ cup rice wine vinegar
½ teaspoon freshly grated orange zest
¼ teaspoon sesame oil
½ teaspoon sea salt
1 medium cucumber peeled, seeded and sliced long ¼ inch thick sticks
1 cup sprouts
2 scallions/green onions, thinly sliced
pickled ginger for garnish

**Directions:**
1. Cook Udon noodles according to package directions, stirring often to keep noodles separated. Rinse with cold water, lifting noodles occasionally to keep them separate.
2. While the noodles are cooking, place the chili flakes into a blender, along with the orange juice, vinegar, and zest and blend to a smooth sauce.
3. Add the oil and sea salt.
4. In a large bowl, mix the noodles, cucumber, sprouts and green onions.
5. Add the orange sauce and toss well, garnish with pickled ginger.
Serve immediately.

## The Perfect Pecan Pesto

**Ingredients:**
1 cup freshly picked basil packed
1/4 cup grated parmesan cheese
1/4 cup extra virgin olive oil
1/8 cup pecans
2 cloves garlic
1/4 teaspoon lemon juice
Sea salt & pepper to taste

**Directions:**
1. Place all of the ingredients in a blender and pulse on low until all of the ingredients are incorporated into a fine green paste.
2. Remove and store in an air-tight container in the refrigerator.

## Pasta with Pecan Pesto

**Ingredients:**
1 (12 oz) box of whole wheat penne
2 Tablespoons olive oil
1 medium zucchini cubed
1 medium sweet red pepper
½ cup carrot sticks
¼ cup portabella mushrooms sliced
1/2 cup of Pecan Pesto– see recipe on page 30

**Directions:**
1. Prepare Penne pasta according to package directions. Drain and set aside.
2. In a large saucepan heat olive oil over medium heat, add the zucchini, sweet red pepper, and carrot sticks.
3. Cook until fork tender.
4. Add the portabella mushrooms and heat for an additional minute.
5. Add the pasta to the pan and mix it with the vegetables.
6. Add the Pecan Pesto into the pasta and vegetables mixing thoroughly.

Serve warm or cold.

## Rachel's Bowtie Pasta

**Ingredients:**
12 oz box of Farfalle pasta prepared
4 Tablespoons olive oil
3 cloves garlic crushed
3/4 cup chopped onion
2 cups sliced zucchini
1/2 cup chopped tomatoes
1/2 cup artichoke hearts sliced
1 teaspoon sea salt
1/2 teaspoon black pepper
1 Tablespoon dried basil
* 4 Tablespoons Blue Cheese for garnish (optional)

**Directions:**
1. In a large saucepan, heat oil over medium heat and add garlic, onion and zucchini. Cook until soft- about 7 minutes.
2. Add tomatoes and heat for two additional minutes.
3. Remove from heat, add artichoke, sea salt, black pepper and basil.
4. Add the pasta and mix well.
5. Serve at room temperature. Garnish with Blue Cheese if desired.

# DIY Pasta

**Ingredients:**
1 1/2 cup whole wheat flour
1/2 cup unbleached flour
1 egg
1/2 teaspoon sea salt
3/4 cup warm water

**Directions:**
1. In a large bowl, mix flour and sea salt. Make a well in the center of the mixture.
2. Add the egg and warm water. Stir to make a stiff dough. Increase water if dough seems too dry.
3. Pat the dough into a ball and turn out onto a lightly floured surface.
4. Knead for 10 to 15 minutes. Cover. Let dough rest for 20 minutes.
5. Roll out dough using rolling pin or pasta machine. Work with a 1/4 of the dough at one time while keeping the rest covered.
6. Roll by hand to 1/16 of an inch thick. Sprinkle with flour if the dough is too wet and sticks to the rolling pin.
7. If you are rolling by machine, continue to feed the pasta through machine stopping at the third to last setting.
8. Cut pasta into desired shapes.
9. Cook fresh noodles in boiling salted water for 3 to 5 minutes. Drain.

| *Recycle-* | *Reduce-* | *Reuse-* |
|---|---|---|
| **Taking leftovers for lunch can save you hundreds of dollars a month for a family of four!**<br><br>**Don't throw old glass jars away, save them to store bulk ingredients in. To get rid of any odors, clean well with soapy water and baking soda.** | **Split bulk purchases with friends or family. Bulk pricing is broken down on the store shelves so you can know what each item costs. This is a great way to save on your grocery bill, while reducing clutter and waste in your pantry.** | **Buy kitchen items second hand. Cookware, kitchen towels and even dishes can be purchased at reasonable prices. Do not purchase non-stick cookware that shows visible damage to the non-stick finish.**<br>**Look for items that are well made and have a lot of life left in them.** |

## The Pennywize Vegetarian

### Low-cost Adaptable Side Dishes

The recipes in this section work great for families where not all of the members are vegetarians. Choose several of these sides to create a veggie– feast and serve them along with a meat choice for those who require it.

## Pico de Gallo Corn

**Ingredients:**
1/2 lb. unsalted butter (2 sticks) softened
1 Tablespoon chopped cilantro
1 1/2 Tablespoon chili powder
1/4 cup grated lime zest
1/2 teaspoon sea salt
1/8 teaspoon black pepper
8 ears corn-1 layer of husks on and silk removed

**Directions:**
1. Combine chili powder with lime zest, sea salt, black pepper and butter in medium bowl; mix well with electric mixer. Chill.
2. Heat grill to medium heat. Remove all but 1 layer of husk from each corn ear. Trim silk from ends.
3. Grill corn 10 to 12 minutes, turning occasionally. Peel off remaining husk and silk.
4. Serve with the chilled butter mixture.

## Summer Squash Medley

**Ingredients:**
2 Tablespoons olive oil
3 cloves garlic crushed
1 cup onion chopped
1 cup bell pepper sliced
3 large yellow or green summer squash (8 cups) sliced 1/4" thick
1 1/2 cup tomato chopped (or a 12 oz can)
2 teaspoons Italian seasoning
1/2 teaspoon sea salt
1 1/2 teaspoon season salt with no MSG
1/2 teaspoon raw sugar
3 cups prepared brown rice

**Directions:**
1. In a large saucepan heat the olive oil and garlic for 2 minutes on medium heat. Add the onion, bell pepper and squash. Cook for 5 minutes.
2. Add the tomatoes Italian seasoning, sea salt, season salt and raw sugar. Cook for 2-3 more minutes until vegetables are all tender.
3. Remove from heat and let rest for 3-5 minutes before serving over rice.

## Green Bean d' Provence

**Ingredients:**
2 Tablespoons Olive Oil
8 Cups fresh string beans
1/4 teaspoon garlic powder
1/2 teaspoon curry powder
1 teaspoon Herbs d' Provence or Italian Seasonings
1/2 teaspoon sea salt
1 1/2 cup diced tomatoes

**Directions:**
1. Heat oil in a large pot over medium heat.
2. Add string beans, garlic powder, curry powder, Herbs d' Provence and sea salt.
3. Cook for five minutes or until color turns darker but beans are still firm.
4. Add tomatoes and cook for five more minutes until tomatoes begin to break down.

## Herbed Chick Peas

**Ingredients:**
1 1/2 Tablespoons vegetable oil
1/2 cup onion sliced
1 teaspoon ground coriander
1/2 teaspoon ground cumin
1/8 teaspoon chili powder
1/2 teaspoon black pepper
1/2 teaspoon sea salt
1- 15 oz can of chickpeas drained
1 teaspoon fresh lemon juice
2 Tablespoons fresh cilantro

**Directions:**
1. Heat oil over medium heat add the onions and cook them for 5 minutes or until slightly browned.
2. Add the coriander, cumin, chili powder, black pepper and sea salt, and cook for about 1 minute.
3. Add the chickpeas and warm through.
4. Remove from heat and stir in lemon juice and fresh cilantro.
Serve warm or at room temperature.

*MSG is a controversial ingredient that has been linked to everything from headaches to death. Considered a safe food additive by the FDA, it may be wiser to avoid eating it.*

# Creamy Coconut Rice

**Ingredients:**
2 Tablespoons Olive Oil
¼ cup chopped peanuts or cashews
½ cup chopped onions
2 cups coconut milk
2 cups water
¼ teaspoon ground ginger
1 (1/2 inch piece fresh ginger peeled and thinly sliced)
1 whole bay leaf
2 cups brown rice rinsed and drained
sea salt to taste

Garnish-
Four boiled eggs
Thinly sliced cucumber
Malaysian Rice Sauce– see recipe below

**Directions:**
1. In a medium saucepan over medium heat, heat the olive oil.
2. Add the chopped nuts and onions and sauté for 1 minute.
3. Stir in the coconut milk, water, ground ginger, fresh ginger, bay leaf, and brown rice.
4. Cover and bring to a boil. Reduce heat and simmer until rice is done. (More water may be added as needed to finish cooking the rice.)
5. Add sea salt to taste and garnish each serving with one sliced egg, cucumber and Malaysian Rice Sauce.

# Spicy Malaysian Rice Sauce

**Ingredients:**
2 Tablespoons vegetable oil
1 medium onion sliced
3 cloves of garlic thinly sliced
3 spring onions thinly sliced
2 teaspoons chili paste
sea salt to taste
3 Tablespoons raw sugar
¼ cup tamarind juice

**Directions:**
1. Heat the vegetable oil in a skillet.
2. Stir in the onions, garlic and spring onions.
3. Cook 1 or 2 minutes until fragrant.
4. Mix in the chili paste and cook for 10 minutes stirring occasionally-If the chili paste is too dry, add a small amount of water.
5. Stir in sea salt, raw sugar, and tamarind juice.
6. Simmer until sauce is thick- about 5 minutes.
7. Remove from heat and serve.

## Whole Wheat Corn Bread

**Ingredients:**
1 cup stone ground corn meal
1 cup whole wheat flour
1 can (14oz) Cream Corn
1/4 cup raw sugar
1 Tablespoon Baking Powder
1 teaspoon Sea Salt
1 egg
1/2 cup Organic Soy Milk

**Directions:**
Preheat oven 375
1. Spray a 9"x9" pan with cooking spray and set aside.
2. In a large bowl sift together dry ingredients.
3. Add the cream corn, egg add soy milk, mix well. The batter should resemble a wet paste.
4. Place mixture into prepared pan and bake for 20-25 minutes or until a toothpick inserted in the center comes out dry.

## Corn Bread Stuffing

**Ingredients:**
4 cups prepared Whole Wheat Corn Bread chunks- see recipe above
2 Tablespoon olive oil
1 cup finely chopped celery
3/4 cup finely chopped bell pepper
1/2 cup finely chopped onion
1 teaspoon season salt without MSG
1/4 teaspoon black pepper
1 Tablespoon sage
1 Tablespoon rosemary

**Directions:**
1. Heat the olive oil in a large pan over medium heat.
2. Add the celery, onions and peppers and cook until moisture forms and the vegetables are translucent.
3. Add the seasonings.
4. Mix in the prepared corn bread and heat until soft and moist.
5. Remove from heat and serve.

*Eating a diet high in nutrient rich foods like whole grains, fresh fruits, vegetables and salads along with moderate exercise can lower your risk of certain cancers by over 50%!*

## Spicy Thai Noodles

**Ingredients:**

3/4 cup creamy peanut butter
1/4 cup coconut milk
2 Tablespoons water
1 Tablespoon tamarind concentrate
2 Tablespoons fresh lime juice
2 Tablespoons Bragg's Liquid Aminos
1 Tablespoon chili sauce
1 Tablespoon minced fresh ginger root
2 cloves garlic, minced
1- 12 oz package of prepared soba noodles
2/3 cup chopped carrot
2/3 cup chopped peppers
1/4 cup chopped peanuts
1/4 cup chopped fresh cilantro
1/4 cup chopped scallions

**Directions:**

1. Prepare soba noodles according to package directions.
2. Place the peanut butter, coconut milk, water, tamarind juice, lime juice, Liquid Aminos, chili sauce, ginger root and garlic in a blender.
3. Toss the noodles and sauce together in a bowl.
4. Top with peanuts, cilantro and scallions.
5. Serve warm or chilled.

## Plantain Cake

**Ingredients:**

3 hard yellow plantains
4 cups water
1 teaspoon sea salt
1 Tablespoon vegetable oil
1- 14 oz can coconut milk
3 teaspoons baking powder

**Directions:**

1. Peel the plantain and cook in water for 30 minutes or until tender.
2. Remove from water and place in a bowl, add the sea salt, vegetable oil coconut milk and baking powder.
3. Blend the mixture with a hand blender until mostly smooth.
4. Transfer to an oiled 9x9 baking dish.
5. Bake in a pre-heated 350 degree oven until slightly golden about 20 minutes.
6. May be served warm or cold.

## Sweet & Sour Hodgepodge

**Ingredients:**
1 (8 oz) can of pineapple chunks in juice
¼ cup packed brown sugar
1 Tablespoon cornstarch
¼ teaspoon ground ginger
¼ cup white vinegar
¼ cup reduced sodium soy sauce
2 Tablespoons of vegetable oil
2 garlic cloves minced
1 medium onion cut into wedges
1 large green pepper cut into 1 inch chunks
1 medium sweet red pepper cut into 1inch chunks
½ cup sliced carrot
½ cup whole nuts- cashews or peanuts
1 (14oz) can kidney beans rinsed and drained
1 (14oz) can black beans rinsed and drained
¾ cups grape tomatoes cut in half

**Directions:**
1. Drain Pineapple (reserving juice) and set pineapple aside.
2. In a bowl, combine the brown sugar, cornstarch and ginger.
3. Add enough water to reserved pineapple juice to measure ½ cup.
4. Stir juice into cornstarch mixture until smooth, add the vinegar and soy sauce, set aside.
5. In a large skillet or wok, heat the vegetable oil and garlic. Add the onion wedges, green pepper, sweet red pepper, carrots and nuts until crisp-tender.
6. Add the beans, tomatoes and reserved pineapple.
7. Cook and stir for 2-3 minutes until heated through.
8. Stir in soy sauce mixture and add the beans. Bring to a boil, cook and stir for 1-2 minutes or until thickened.
9. Served alone, over rice or noodles.

## Pecan Pesto Potatoes

**Ingredients:**
8 cups thinly sliced potatoes
4 oz Pecan Pesto -recipe on page 30
1 teaspoon sea salt
1/2 teaspoon black pepper
1/2 cup soy milk

**Directions:**
Preheat oven to 375.
Place the potatoes in a baking dish. Season with sea salt and black pepper and mix in the pesto. Smooth the layers of potatoes evenly in the pan and add the soymilk. Cover and bake until potatoes are fork tender about 30 minutes.

## Meaty Vegetarian Dishes

Whatever your preference- every vegetarian can eat meat! Well, meat analogs. Have you tried them? There are so many on the market that are right for you. Enjoy them to add a little texture and variation to your diet plan.

## Jamaican Pouches

**Ingredients:**
2 Tablespoons vegetable oil
1 1/2 cup chopped onion
6 cloves garlic, minced
1 Tablespoon finely chopped fresh ginger
1 bag of Grounds
1 pound ripe tomatoes chopped
1 jalapeño pepper, seeded and finely chopped
2 teaspoons dried thyme
1/4 teaspoon ground turmeric
3/4 teaspoon ground cumin
3/4 teaspoon ground allspice
1/2 teaspoon ground green or black cardamom
1 Tablespoon finely chopped parsley
1 1/2 teaspoon sea salt
Freshly ground black pepper
One batch of Flaky Baked Empanada Dough– see recipe on page 40

**Directions:**
Preheat oven to 400 degrees
1. In a large saucepan heat the oil.
2. Add in the onion, minced garlic, chopped fresh ginger. Heat for 3 minutes.
3. Add the bag of grounds, tomatoes, jalapeno pepper and spices. Cook the ingredients thoroughly for 5 minutes then remove from heat.
4. Divide empanada dough into 10 balls and roll them out into a flat circle.
5. Place filling on one half of circle and fold the dough over.
6. Seal the edges with water and crimp with a fork.
7. Place on an ungreased baking sheet and cook in a 400 oven until golden brown.

*Vegetarians maintain a diet consisting of plant based foods but will also eat foods produced without harming the animal such as eggs, milk, butter, yogurt and cheese. Vegetarians also eat honey but not gelatin or marshmallows as they are produced with animal protein.*

## Flaky Baked Empanada Dough

**Ingredients:**
1 ½ cup unbleached flour
1 cup wheat flour
½ Tablespoon baking powder
1 teaspoon sea salt
½ cup vegetable shortening or cold coconut oil
½ cup soymilk

**Directions:**
1. Combine dry ingredients in a bowl.
2. Cut the vegetable shortening or coconut oil into dry ingredients until it resembles bread crumbs.
3. Add soymilk and mix to form dough.
4. Shape dough into a ball and knead 10 times.
5. Cover bowl and let the dough rest for one half hour.
6. Make fist size balls of dough.
7. Roll them out and fill according to recipe directions and bake at 375 degrees until golden brown.

## Jammin' Yam Casserole

**Ingredients:**
1 batch Jamaican Pouch Filling Prepared– recipe on page 39
6 cups cooked sweet potatoes
1-14 oz can of sweetened condensed milk
2 teaspoons cinnamon
1 teaspoon ground ginger
2 Tablespoons vegetable oil
2 eggs beaten

**Directions:**
Preheat oven to 350 degrees
1. In a large bowl, beat the sweet potatoes, condensed milk, cinnamon, ginger, vegetable oil and eggs until fluffy.
2. In a casserole dish, layer the filling on the bottom and the sweet potato on top. Smooth and place in the oven.
3. Bake until the sweet potatoes begin to stiffen and brown about 30 minutes.

*Vegans maintain a strict diet excluding animal produced ingredients which would include honey, sugar processed through bone char, eggs and animal milk.*

## A Bowl of Red

**Ingredients:**
1 Tablespoon vegetable oil
1 large yellow onion, diced
1 green bell pepper, seeded and diced
1 red bell pepper, seeded and diced
1/4 cup TVP (Texturized Vegetable Protein) Flakes
(prepared according to package directions)
1 cup sliced celery
2 cloves garlic, minced
28-oz. can crushed tomatoes
15-oz. can red kidney beans, drained
15-oz. can stewed tomatoes, diced
4 teaspoon chili powder
1 Tablespoon dried oregano
2 1/2 teaspoon ground cumin
1 teaspoon paprika
1 teaspoon salt
2 teaspoon bottled hot sauce
1/2 teaspoon ground black pepper

**Directions:**
1. Heat oil in large saucepan. Add onion, bell peppers, TVP, celery and garlic. Cook for 6 to 8 minutes.
2. Stir in crushed tomatoes, beans, stewed tomatoes and seasonings; bring to a simmer.
3. Cook uncovered over low heat, stirring occasionally, 25 to 30 minutes.
4. Remove from heat; let stand 5 to 10 minutes before serving.

## Big Momma Biscuits

**Ingredients:**
1 ½ cup unbleached flour
½ cup wheat flour
1 Tablespoon baking powder
1 teaspoon sea salt
1 Tablespoon raw sugar
1/3 cup vegetable shortening or butter
1 cup organic soy milk

**Directions:**
Preheat oven to 400
1. In a large bowl, whisk together the dry ingredients. Cut in the shortening until the mixture resembles coarse meal. Stir in soy milk until the dough pulls away from the side of the bowl.
2. Turn out onto a floured surface and GENTLY knead 20 times, pat or roll dough out to about ½ inch thickness.
3. Cut into twelve pieces with a sharp knife or pizza cutter and place on an ungreased baking sheet. Bake for 13-15 minutes until edges begin to brown.

# Big Momma Biscuits & Sausage Gravy

**Ingredients:**
1 batch Big Momma Biscuits prepared– recipe on page 41
2 Tablespoons oil
1/2 teaspoon chopped garlic
1 cup chopped onion
1/2 cup chopped bell peppers
1- 12 oz bag of Morning Star ® Sausage Crumbles
1 teaspoon sea salt
1/2 teaspoon black pepper
1 teaspoon rubbed sage
1/2 teaspoon thyme
2 Tablespoons whole wheat flour
2 cups soy milk

**Directions:**
1. Heat oil over medium heat in a large skillet, add garlic, onion and peppers. Cook for 3 minutes.
2. Add the crumbles, sea salt, black pepper, sage and thyme. Cook until crumbles are soft.
3. Sprinkle on the wheat flour and mix in well.
4. Add the soy milk and stir constantly to keep lumps from forming.
5. Heat to thicken, remove from heat and serve.

# Meatless Meatballs & Gravy

**Ingredients:**
2 Tablespoons of vegetable oil
3/4 Cup Sliced Bell Peppers
3/4 Cup Sliced Onion
2 Packages of Quorn ® Brand "Meatballs"
1 teaspoon season salt– MSG free
1 teaspoon garlic powder
1 teaspoon curry powder
1/2 teaspoon sea salt-MSG free
1 1/2 teaspoon Italian seasonings
2 Cups Water
3 teaspoons Corn Starch dissolved in 1/3 Cup Water

**Directions:**
1. In a large pan heat the olive oil. Add the bell peppers and onions. Cook for 3 minutes until fragrant. Add the Meatless meatballs to the pot and continue to cook. Add the seasonings and stir well.
2. Add 2 cups of water and simmer for 5 minutes. Add the water/cornstarch mixture by slowly stirring it in. Return to simmer.
3. Cook until thickened, remove from heat and serve.

## Save Money By Making Your Own Snacks & Specialty Drinks

The recipes in this section will teach you how save a bundle by and make better choices for your occasional snacking.

## Veggie Chips

**Ingredients:**
Any hard root vegetable sliced very thin.
(Sweet Potatoes, Potatoes, Carrots, Beets, Hicama)
Cooking spray oil

**Directions:**
1. Preheat oven to 425.
2. Place thinly sliced vegetables on a lightly sprayed cookie sheet.
3. Place in oven and bake until crisp and dry.
5. Time will vary according to thickness of vegetable slices but generally allow between 5-10 minutes.

## Tortilla Chips

**Ingredients:**
package flour tortillas or 1 package corn tortillas
Cooking spray/ oil
sea salt

**Directions:**
Preheat oven to 350
1. Spray a very light coating of oil on one side of each tortilla.
2. Stack the tortillas, greased side up, in an even pile and cut the stack in half, quarters and then into eighths.
3. Separate the pieces and arrange them oiled side up on a baking sheet.
4. Bake for about 10 minutes or until they are crisp and just beginning to brown slightly.
5. Remove from oven and salt lightly.

*Pescetarians maintain a diet that is, in many cases, similar to that of the ovo-lacto vegetarian but also includes seafood in their diet.*

## Salsa de Patty

**Ingredients:**
3 tomatoes grilled
5 hot peppers grilled
1/2 medium onion
2 cloves garlic
1/4 cup water
1 teaspoon sea salt

**Directions:**
Combine all ingredients in a blender and pulse until it reaches desired consistency.
May be kept refrigerated for up to one week.

## Creamy Coconut Bananas

**Ingredients:**
4 large under ripe bananas (peeled and sliced diagonally about ¾ inch thick)
2 Tablespoons butter or butter substitute
2 Tablespoons brown sugar
1 teaspoon lime juice
1 (12 oz) can of coconut milk
2 Tablespoons toasted coconut*

**Directions:**
1. In a saucepan over medium heat, place the butter or butter substitute, and brown sugar to melt.
2. Add the bananas and lime juice. Cook the bananas until they begin to soften.
3. Add the coconut milk and lower heat and simmer for 2 minutes stirring often to coat the bananas.
4. Remove from heat and top with toasted coconut. Serve warm.

\* To toast coconut, place on a dry pan and heat over medium. Stir occasionally as the coconut begins to brown. Once it is slightly brown, but not dark. Remove from pan and set aside.

*Pollotarians restrict their diet to vegetables and birds, such as chicken, turkey and ducks. Some will also eat dairy.*

# Sticky Brown Rice with Mango

**Ingredients:**
1 ripe mango sliced*

Rice:
1 cup brown rice (short grained preferred)
1 ¾ cup water
¼ cup coconut milk
1 Tablespoon raw shredded coconut

Sauce:
½ cup coconut milk
½ cup raw sugar
½ teaspoon sea salt

**Directions:**
1. In a saucepan, combine the rice, water and coconut milk. Bring to a boil, reduce heat, cover and simmer- stirring occasionally until rice is tender. Remove from heat and add the shredded coconut.
2. In the meantime combine the ingredients for the sauce in a bowl, whisk together and set aside.
3. To serve, place the rice on a platter, pour the sauce on and add the mango slices on top.

* Mangoes should be plump and heavy for their size. A ripe mango will slightly indent when pressed with your thumb. Avoid mangoes that are soft, mushy or have brown spots. To slice a mango, lay it on its side and cut beside the ridge to avoid the large stone in the center. Peel each section and slice.

# 1-2-3 Peanut Butter Cookies

**Ingredients:**
1 egg
1 cup Peanut Butter
1 cup Brown Sugar

**Directions:**
1. Preheat oven to 350 degrees.
2. Combine all ingredients in a mixing bowl.
3. Roll into walnut size balls and place on a cookie sheet.
4. Press flat in a criss-cross fashion with the tines of a fork.
5. Bake until firm and slightly brown.

# Black Bean Blender Brownies

**Ingredients:**
1- 15 oz can black beans rinsed and drained
3 eggs
3 Tablespoons Vegetable Oil
1/4 cup Cocoa Powder
1/8 teaspoon Sea Salt
1 teaspoon Vanilla Extract
3/4 cup Raw Sugar
1 teaspoon freshly ground
Canela* ( Mexican Cinnamon)
2 Ground Green Cardamom Pods

* Canela is usually found in plastic bags for around $1.00 in ethnic grocery stores. It has a sharper flavor and a softer texture than other types of cinnamon. Although Canela is recommended for this recipe any form of cinnamon can be used.

**Directions:**
Preheat oven to 350.
1. Lightly oil an 8x8 baking dish and set to the side.
2. Place all ingredients in a blender and blend until smooth.
3. Pour mixture into prepared baking dish.
4. Bake until the top is dry and the edges pull away from the side of the pan about 30 minutes.

# Almond Masala Chai

**Ingredients:**
3 Cups Water
4 Cloves
2 Cardamom Pods
1 Cinnamon Stick Crushed
1 teaspoon Ground Ginger
1/8 teaspoon Black Pepper
1/2 Cup Vanilla Almond Milk– recipe on page 15
2 Tablespoons Raw Sugar
2 Black or Green Tea Bags

**Directions:**
1. Place all of the ingredients in a saucepan and heat until just boiling.
2. Remove from heat and let sit for 5 minutes.
3. Strain and enjoy hot or cold.

# Hibiscus Spritzer

**Ingredients:**
1 cup water
2 Tablespoons Hibiscus Flowers
2 Tablespoon Raw Sugar or honey
Mineral or Seltzer Water

**Directions:**
1. Combine all ingredients in a saucepan and bring ingredients to a boil.
2. Remove from heat and steep for 10 minutes.
3. Strain and refrigerate for 1 hour.
4. Pour 1/3 mixture into 2/3 seltzer or mineral water to serve.

# Ginger Honey Tisane

**Ingredients:**
2 quarts water
2 cups fresh lemon juice
1 cup honey
1- 3 inch piece of ginger peeled and thinly sliced

**Directions:**
1. In a large saucepan, combine all of the ingredients and bring them to a simmer over medium heat.
2. Stir to dissolve the honey.
3. Remove from heat and cover for 15 minutes.
4. Strain, serve hot or cold.

*Flexitarians are individuals who eat a mostly vegetarian (ovo-lacto) diet but occasionally eat meat. This is usually the first step to becoming a full- fledged vegetarian and is also known as a "semi-vegetarianism."*

# Resources

**Atlantic Spice Co.-** Bulk/ Wholesale Herbs & Spices www.AtlanticSpice.com

**Cutco USA-** Knives with Forever Guarantee - www.cutco.com

**Eat Cleaner- Fruit & Veggie Wipes** (pg 11)- www.eatcleaner.com

**Full Circle Home LLC-Circle Brush** (pg 11)- available on Amazon.com

**Good Bye Detergent-** Spaghetti Scrubber/ Environmentally Responsible Cleaning Products- www.GoodByeDetergent.com

**Kitchen aid-** Small Kitchen Appliances- www. kitchenaid.com

**PCRM-** Vegetarian Eating Guide, Recipes & Information on overcoming illness through good nutrition- www.PCRM.org

**Protect A Pan-** Pan Protectors- www.protectapan.com- Available at Bed Bath and Beyond

**Skrub'a** (pg 11)- Potato Gloves- www.fabrikatorsusa.com- Available at Dillard's

**Xtreme Fuel Treatment-** Increases mileage, reduces emissions by 33%, extends engine life and performance. www.YouCanSaveAtThePump.com

## About The Author

Andréa Renée Frayser is a graduate of The Herbal Healer Academy where she studied Holistic Nutrition, Herbal Pharmacology and Naturopathy (Natural Medicine). She in an internationally recognized, award winning, vegan product formulator and is the Founder of Balsam of Gilead Natural Wellness.

Andrea works tirelessly educating and lecturing on the importance of feeding the body "from the inside out and the outside in". She was inspired to write *The Pennywize Vegetarian* by her students and colleagues who were looking for a practical, no non-sense guide to feeding their families healthier meals without sacrificing taste, time or money.

Andrea enjoys cooking these and many other recipes for friends and family in her home in Hagerstown, MD which she shares with her husband, three children, Mary Muffin (the Diva Kitty) and "Broke Bunny" also known as Goshen the Great.

A Note of Thanks...
There are so many people who have encouraged, supported and inspired me during the writing of this book, and in my heart and prayers I have thanked you more times than you could know.

There are a few that stand out in my heart as "the cheerleaders of my life" and I would like to take a few moments to thank them formerly:

To my sister Marcia. Thank you for never telling me to "stop dreaming" and thank you for following your own unspoken advice.

To Lena Simone, Proverbs 17:17 says it all.

Additionally, I would like to say a special "Thanks!" to my parents Arbury Russell Jones and Constance Givens– Jones, and to my *very* large extended family which includes Yvonne "Grandma" Timbers.

My gratitude also extends to the businesses who sell *The Pennywize Vegetarian* as well as the ones that shared their products, ideas and services with me while I was researching this book. I wish you all the best.

Finally– Thank YOU for your support.

www.ingramcontent.com/pod-product-compliance
Lightning Source LLC
Chambersburg PA
CBHW041754040426
42446CB00001B/26

mind and as you can see this is the result of what kept coming to mind.

I pray that this book will help those of you that may need that little extra push to get started with your life as God has planned it for you. For each of us there is a calling on our lives to give to the world something that God has placed on the inside of all of us. We all have a destiny that God wants us to fulfill here on earth. It is up to us to find that true destiny that is within. Never say never, it is never too late to get started walking in your destiny. This may be just the time that God wants you to get started, you never know. God knew when and where He wanted you to be born. Take what you have or whatever you may not have and use it to your advantage. There is always a silver lining to every cloud.

However His plan for us is to allow us to become productive in every area of our lives. God never intended on any negative outcome to surface in our lives, that was not His plan. His plan was and still is for us to live on earth just as if we are in Heaven with Him.

Weather you know it or not we can live that way if we would just change our outlook about the Kingdom of God. To renew your mind is to change the way you think. In order to change the way you think you must learn the right way to think.

As you continue to read this book you will learn some of the concepts of the right way of thinking. I pray that God opens your understanding to what has been written in this book.